# Palpitations And Nerve Tracing

D. D. Palmer

# Kessinger Publishing's Rare Reprints

## Thousands of Scarce and Hard-to-Find Books on These and other Subjects!

- Americana
- Ancient Mysteries
- Animals
- Anthropology
- Architecture
- Arts
- Astrology
- Bibliographies
- Biographies & Memoirs
- Body, Mind & Spirit
- Business & Investing
- Children & Young Adult
- Collectibles
- Comparative Religions
- Crafts & Hobbies
- Earth Sciences
- Education
- Ephemera
- Fiction
- Folklore
- Geography
- Health & Diet
- History
- Hobbies & Leisure
- Humor
- Illustrated Books
- Language & Culture
- Law
- Life Sciences
- Literature
- Medicine & Pharmacy
- Metaphysical
- Music
- Mystery & Crime
- Mythology
- Natural History
- Outdoor & Nature
- Philosophy
- Poetry
- Political Science
- Science
- Psychiatry & Psychology
- Reference
- Religion & Spiritualism
- Rhetoric
- Sacred Books
- Science Fiction
- Science & Technology
- Self-Help
- Social Sciences
- Symbolism
- Theatre & Drama
- Theology
- Travel & Explorations
- War & Military
- Women
- Yoga
- *Plus Much More!*

**We kindly invite you to view our catalog list at:
http://www.kessinger.net**

THIS ARTICLE WAS EXTRACTED FROM THE BOOK:

The Chiropractor

BY THIS AUTHOR:

D. D. Palmer

ISBN 156459775X

READ MORE ABOUT THE BOOK AT OUR WEB SITE:

http://www.kessinger.net

OR ORDER THE COMPLETE
BOOK FROM YOUR FAVORITE STORE

ISBN 156459775X

# Palpation and Nerve Tracing.

The chiropractor determines the position of bones, more especially those of the vertebral column, the condition and pathway of subdermal nerves, by palpation; this is known as physical diagnosis. This examination is performed by a discriminating touch of the fingers which, directed by knowledge and the skill acquired by continued application, become very sensitive. The truth of the science, the correctness of the art and the reasonableness of its philosophy are demonstrated thereby.

Nerve tracing is an art. The systematic application of knowledge regarding the condition of nerves in health and disease, observation, study, experience and skill acquired by constant practice, has resulted in determining certain principles and facts which enable us to determine the luxated joints, which by their displacement cause more or less nerve-tension, variation of functions, conditions known as disease.

The art of palpation to determine the condition of subcutaneous organs has been used for centuries by medical practitioners. The art of nerve-tracing is of recent date, your teacher was the first to practice it.

The chiropractor should trace sensitive, swollen, longitudially contracted nerves, for the purpose of locating their impingement and tension. By palpation he determines the one or more spinous processes which project posterior of the normal outline. The projection of the displaced spinous process is in the direction of the bend; in the cervical it is anterior, in the dorsal posterior and ventral in the lumbar. In a practice of twenty-five years I have only known one case of reversed kyphosis and lordosis which I relieved by adjusting the twelfth dorsal. There are three vertebrae which may be considered as stationary, the axis, the first dorsal and the sacrum. There is no better way to locate the cause of disease, or demonstrate to a prospective patient how bones and nerves are related to each other and why such relationship accounts for health and disease, than by palpation and nerve-tracing.

By palpation and nerve-tracing the chiropractor can often determine the organ and the innervating subdermal nerves affected. Nerves in their normal condition are not sensitive to pressure; those in the teeth are not affected by cold or hot, sweet or sour ingesta.

By a unique movement the nerve which is unduly stretched, because of being impinged against, or stretched by a displaced bone of the neuro-skeleton, is returned to its normal tension, normal vibration, normal temperature and normal functionating.

Chiropractors demonstrate the correctness of Dr. Dunglison's statement in his dictionary, "Irritation is indicated by tenderness on pressure over the spinous process of one or more vertebrae or parts of the sides of the spine."

Chiropractors are demonstrating upon living subjects, no cadavers, no vivisection, that there are nerve fibers which have not been noticed by anatomists. Nerve tracing explains this unexplainable explanation of "vicarious commutation," or substitution.

A number of theories have been advanced to explain the process of heredity, the transmission of acquired characteristics, the perpetuation of ancestral distinguishing traits and qualities, including the inheritance of disease from ancestors. One of which is that germinal continuity, minute particles are given off from all cells of the body and collected in the reproductive, generative, living, active basis of all animal organizations; they represent all of the body characteristics, both heredity and acquired.

Medical men believe that the cause of diseases originate outside the body, or are generated within the body. Those outside are, traumatic, heat, cold, poisons and living organisms such as bacteria and animal parasites. Those "originated within the body are less definitely known." "The self-poisoning is designated auto-intoxication."

Pneumonia, diptheria, typhoid fever, measles, mumps, whooping cough and rheumatism are among those diseases acquired by inheritance, transmitted from parent to offspring, physical or mental qualities conveyed from ancestors to their progeny. This theory includes the doubling and multiplication of the vital units of the future individual, which accounts for the variation of form, physical and mental qualities, including the transference of disease. Speculation based on such assumed hypothesis necessarily falls to the ground, as no sharp distinction exists between germ-cells and somatic (pertaining to the wall of the body or the body as a whole) cells.

The above named diseases are classed as those of heredity, whose duration is considered self-limited, are readily relieved by chiropractic adjustments.

Conscious intelligence is the observation of impressions received through the sensory organs of sight, hearing, smell, taste, and touch. To these may be added perception, apprehension, recognition, understanding, discernment and appreciation of our physical surroundings, and these are increased by occult intuition and spiritual instinct, the ability of knowing and the power of acting without the assistance of reason.

Intuitive sense is modified by imagination and memory, by the discriminating qualities of intensification, by the condition of tone and the variation from the standard of health. Modified intuitive sense varies the actions of instinctive consciousness.

Intuitive knowing and instinctive action are determined by organic habits and unconscious sensation without thought or volition.

Instinct is immediate in action without the process of reason.

Intuition consists of knowing without reasoning from cause to effect, direct immediate perception without reasoning.

Instinct is a natural, inherited impulse, unassisted by a reasoning conception of that which occasions or effects a result.

Intuition is the ability of knowing without reason, the immediate perception of truth without conscious investigation, or assigning rational causes for their existence.

Instinct is an inward unconscious principle in man and the lower animals, an involuntary prompting which causes mental or physical action without individual experience or a distinct apprehension of the end to be accomplished, an innate tendency to perform a special action in a distinctive way when the necessity occurs.

Intuitive belief, intuitive judgment and intuitive knowledge are qualities due to direct perception, the result of inward consciousness. Intuition may be mystical, perceptional, intellectual or moral. We may have mystical vision, spiritual perception and direct intellectual apprehension.

Hexiology is the science of habits. A habit is a tendency to perform the same spontaneous action under similar circumstances. Habit applies to individuals, instinct to ancestors. Habits acquired through our ancestors are known as instinct.

Organic habits may be acquired by the physical organism during the life of an individual or of a race. The system of bodily processes of the physiological organism has been acquired through past generations.

Constant practice, frequent repetition, habitual custom, confirms habit until it becomes a function. Mental or organic habits are acquired through the education of the nervous system.

In biology our environments are the aggregate of all the external conditions and influences affecting the life and development of an organism. In a measure we regulate our surroundings, giving but little thought of individual and organic habits. Pernicious habits may become fastened upon the human will, weaken vitality and bore tunnels through the reservoirs of force and character. Self-respect and restraint of passions are as essential to longevity as prophylaxis, the science and art of retaining the health. Besides that are dangerous must be shunned; the mind must be kept wholesome.

Every time we think, each time we act, a record is made. Each repetition of a thought, each performance of an act deepens the groove of habit, mental or physical; it renders the next similar impulse or movement more automatic until in time the nervous system becomes like a phonograph disk; without apparent consciousness we find ourselves guilty of repetition. Habits become our master and we its slave.

Pure air, clean water, unadulterated food and thoughts free from error and vulgarism will form cleanly habits of mind and body.

Chiropractors should comprehend the principle of reflex action.

Reflex is the bounding back, the return of an impulse. A reflex action is one executed without our will, one performed and directed by that intelligence which controls the sympathetic nervous system, the nerves of organic life. An involuntary movement of an organ or part of the body resulting from an impression carried by a sensory or afferent to a subordinate center, and then sent back by an efferent nerve to some place at or near the source of irritation is known as reflex action.

All acts performed without brain function are known as reflex actions. The involuntary brushing a fly from the face, or the attempt to move away from an annoyance when tickeled with a feather are examples. In reflex acts, a person does not think before he acts; he acts before he thinks. The nervous impulse comes from the outside and returned, is acted upon without going to the cerebrum. As it were, the message is short-circuited back to the surface by motor nerves, without having reached the thinking centers. Automatic acts are accomplished without thinking. By training the acts have become automatic. Habits are really acquired reflex actions. Habit trains certain nerve centers.

Reflex action is the bounding back of an impulse; the conveyance of an impression from the central system, and its transmission back to the periphery through a motor nerve. The amount of function depends upon the renitency, the impulsive force obtained by the bounding back, the reflex action.

A reflex pathway is the route taken by an impulse; it includes the afferent nerve, the nerve-center and the efferent nerve.

A reflex center is any ganglionic center where a sensory impression is changed into a motor impulse.

Sneezing and the involuntary sniffing of an odor, whether pleasant or unpleasant, are reflex actions. Coughing and choking may be produced by tickling the pharynx, reflex actions, the performance of functions by the controlling intelligence without using the encephalon. Accumulated urine and feces call for micturition and defecation, reflex action.

An enlarged, contracted, sensitive nerve may in reality be only a nerve fiber which may leave a nerve (a bundle of fibers) and enter another; thus, we trace many nerve fibers from their exit at the spinal foramen to their destination, or vice versa, nerve filaments which have not been recognized by anatomists.

Be careful to make a distinction between palpation, perceiving by the sense of touch and palpitation, rapid pulsation of the heart.

CPSIA information can be obtained
at www.ICGtesting.com
Printed in the USA
383554LV00018B/117